COLUMBIA COLLEGE CHICAGO

3 2711 00126 6729

In this contemplative and lyrical collection, Dan Machlin suggests that one solution to the classic mind/body problem is to first acknowledge the body as truly other. Rather than romanticizing or dissecting, getting cozy or visceral, he reawakens us to the mystery of embodiment through a coolly distanced reinvention of the epistolary form. The tone of these letters is elegant and almost elegiac, austere yet oddly moving. In "a country / where sentimentality / has all but faded," the body continues to haunt and fascinate us.

— ELAINE EQUI

The salutation "Dear," Dear Someone, already anachronistic, along with the stamp and the signature. No one is now present to epistelatory intimacy. And yet, here is a book of poems: *Dear Body*. As if the mind and its linguistic dream were unable to sever itself from an address, unable to become an anonymous slate. Dan Machlin upholds the singular clarities of speaking from one body to another. A body of knowledge, for example. A body of endurance. Brilliant, fierce, and spare, these poems bring us, line by line, into a new apprehension of what we are all too ready to rescind. "Is it sufficient that the body at times / can be thought to overwrite the purity of consciousness?" The answer is both personal and resonant: "because I'm scared / about nothing being done."

— ANN LAUTERBACH

These poems are full of searing ebulliences and secret concavities in which a reader might find herself unclothed of her notions. The body finds its lover in itself, we touch the blue glass twice in the same place — these interior motions by which we learn "constancy and boredom" — and the poem unfolds an intimacy so private I feel denuded. It is the most refreshing stripping, like a mist of cool water in a thirsty hour. If ever there were a humane genome embedded in language's possibilities, Machlin has found it and is tapping out the words on those beads.

— ELENI SIKELIANOS

W9-CLN-859

AUG 7 2008

AUG   7 2002

DEAR BODY:

DEAR BODY:
DAN MACHLIN

COLUMBIA COLLEGE LIBRARY
600 S. MICHIGAN AVENUE
CHICAGO, IL 60605

UGLY DUCKLING PRESSE
BROOKLYN, NY

DEAR BODY:
© DAN MACHLIN 2007

UGLY DUCKLING PRESSE
ISBN-13: 978-1-933254-29-6

DISTRIBUTED TO THE TRADE BY
SPD / SMALL PRESS DISTRIBUTION
1341 SEVENTH STREET
BERKELEY, CA 94710
WWW.SPDBOOKS.ORG

ALSO AVAILABLE DIRECTLY FROM UDP
AND THROUGH OUR PARTNER BOOKSTORES

Library of Congress Cataloging-in-Publication Data

Machlin, Dan.
  Dear body / Dan Machlin. -- 1st ed.
     p. cm.
  ISBN 978-1-933254-29-6 (pbk. : alk. paper)
  I. Title.
  PS3613.A27253D43 2007
  811'.6--dc22
                                2007034423

THIS BOOK WAS MADE POSSIBLE IN PART BY A "FACE OUT" GRANT
FROM THE JEROME FOUNDATION AND THE COUNCIL OF LITERARY
MAGAZINES AND PRESSES

FIRST EDITION 2007
PRINTED IN THE USA

UGLY DUCKLING PRESSE
THE OLD AMERICAN CAN FACTORY
232 THIRD STREET #E-002
BROOKLYN, NEW YORK 11215

WWW.UGLYDUCKLINGPRESSE.ORG

FOR SERENA

CONTENTS

DEAR BODY:

ANTEBODIES

BEAUTIFUL LINEAR BODIES

DEAR BODY:

If this is the year of clarity, it is the year of the priest's death. I must kill him to become him — a cluster bomb of a man — tiny beautiful droplets of a child's leg blown to nothingness.

I have word clusters to give you — prayers hung from flowering trees in Japanese panel painting.

Suppose if this is snow, I am never with you. We were in this house see and living our separate lives but never meeting.

If only I could give you the accident
and you could give me your non-acceptance of the event.

I know how we can do it.
Fuse the nuclei — no plant bulbs on the terrace.

No missed opportunities:
to run, to sunbathe, run
& sunbathe.

I was thinking
of creating a museum of symbols —
symbols of our hagiography.

So far in this insignificance I can't say how I left you. How I felt the last dance of a pulse — a cloud and — as a cliché mid-sentence — proverbial stuttering.

I was with you growing inside —
some memory of me not there.

The darkness, a lovely fugue.
"So sorry," I said, for a lifetime of sorries.

I wanted to write a perfect vignette/
description — perfect fusion of memory and encyclopedic entry:

Symbols: an alleyway,
the comfort of exhaustion —

There's something in being taken out of the game altogether.

I dreamt of being draped in luxurious velvet and the loneliness would almost seem noble — necessary.

This is what the job entailed. This is
what I was born into and being born into do not shirk from.

Lately I have been feeling estranged from you again. Doubtful
you ever existed.

Cut off a finger to see if you would notice, but the blood said nothing and I just stood there moments with an open mouth.

When I was small, I lay in a field and imagined the earth spun when the clouds moved.

Remember that woman on lithium who used to stop for a moment and stare into the trees — she said it was a standing meditation (but admitted she had to pee often).

It was you, wasn't it, who was anti-fashion — out came the flannel shirts on dusty hangers in the forsaken closet.

And what of Italy? They wash their silken blacks in rainwater.

Traced my finger over your surveillance mechanism. So if that was the device, the device didn't work.

Searched for you in discos — but not before the union of horrific assumptions skipped a beat and came out all wrong.

You may find that accepting this inevitable fact about your life will not be easy.

Herein I describe the state of being delimited by this perfunctory container. Although you held your hand over my heart I could not believe your touch.

No strike that insane cliché and replace it with an equation. I led them down a false path to discover the humane genome.

Meanwhile you were hiding underneath the table. At one time, they too could assemble you out of grass — an abandoned rug and decaying vegetables.

We prayed to your effigy like to a beautiful library book you wanted to steal — the perfect never-noticed crime.

Many years later indexing doubts about your presence you uncover lost plans for some extreme city.

Or you as your own forbidden lover who meets yourself late at night in a forgotten deco motel.

A brief conversation about ephemera (each word drenched with sexual potential).

You know, I've never believed in your hope. So somehow the limbs attached to a trunk of meat and toes a face lips that say a nose balding teeth barely —

O how this house whispers beneath the dinner table!

Whether my mind to my knee or a chest as hollow as a creek bed, these are the questions I am always asking, trying to mutter an answer to.

If there was one popular tree on my property, it was the dream tree — arms spread out in full growth, no shading here.

But what do I know — I was a city boy raised in the sky. Now I am wandering into the eternal justification some call lethargy.

This body, he said (as if this specific body had a house, a housing).

No, we were not just pleasant beings gazing into the sun, slightly tired and not yet hungry, having eaten lunch much too late.

And who is this *we* anyway — I was alone — tabulating the pros and cons of my history, sitting beside the ache in one's arrogance meets devastation —

this
non-man, a rupture.

In the beginning, the land tore itself apart in volcanic ebulliences and simultaneously collapsed inward into tectonic concavity.

It was I who was being carried — a
saint in a glass box, lord of

Liberty Island,
rabbi of abandoned parks.

I did not try to curry favor with the locals, though they tied me to the grammar with their hammers.

Insignificance, a pre-populated field whose minor chord inspired complaints about lost wages.

It was as if, here I was in you, my body, waging devastation on a foreign body — deformed bodies of state.

We tried to type the pattern out. Each of the letters so perfectly repeating that I stored them on separate index cards —

As if to tell time through lack of ego — as if an envelope to be discovered later after death — a kiss in a movie.

I was never a professional.

I would tell you I'm a writer but always unwrite houses.

I too have been there to the ship addressing topics.

How specifically I unheard this story you would look sad in:

on May 2nd remember — the rainy day, the day of shadowman —

I was going to save you part of a brioche but you were late and I ate it all myself and you never knew it existed.

I undressed for the 10,000th time and you didn't laugh but instead we examined each other as separate entities.

"Hell," I said, "I'm done with writing I want to hold your life in."

There was a time when I would suggest an expurgation — but you would not be open to an expurgation —

There was a fleeting feeling of confusion in my text — but when you came around again you wrote a lengthy text in your own right.

Dear Body:

I never had faith that this letter-writing campaign would undermine our intimacy.

Instead I would buy pieces of land near "forever-wild" forests in the hope that I might never again need to experience closeness.

Not, that is to say, closeness itself, but rather the concept of "closeness," as when Julliette died and there was this unhealthy silence.

A hush fell over our tomb and expressed outward over the meadow and gray buildings.

Your critique of our correspondence as some sort of proto-self, rejecting urgency of the world and all outward responsibilities, ignores many households with only one person, millions who seek new forms and patterns so we are not collectively digressing. I was saying this over a glass of wine ignoring your condemnation based on the inevitability of my behavior (or as you might put it "pre-programmed characteristics"). I myself have surfed the old forms tried living with humans written poems about your incredible eyes for instance and the fourth eye that enters at dusk or when meditating on in-betweens laughing at nothing in particular.

DEAR BODY:

You write:

they proclaimed the house was no longer a dwelling

but we slept there often enough to film ourselves
                    itemizing each moment with a dash

I am forever cleaning you away as if dash
dash —
the pencil breaks

you were twirling it adeptly during the meeting
the pencil — other worlds I thought —

you are here and I am thinking no typing — *you are
not these words*

Look since I believed once

(living between place and absence,
definition and the occult)

and you housed me on these terms

I dedicate this operation to
doesn't matter —

manifestos —
this use of a song,

an opening, an architecture —

Materials, whether they be
environmentally responsible

      or reckless

I am not the recorder of this
but simply the set-up

going along with a bass beat curious piano line

early fatigue

and the information in the rare disease database

I'm broken up/
can't hold

this forced opposition
between constancy and boredom

Perhaps a blue glass —

object obsession

Touching it and then
touching it in the same place

Hello again my little word, the smallest explanation.

Bird that took over our apartment.

We were always speaking so small it snowed
I thought or the occult of
having each of us in this place.

Stop.

This was supposed to be a simple meeting
of two souls. *This was supposed to be*
a simple meeting of two souls.

This doubling I exposed you to

     under the blue starlight and you explained "please, no more memories."
So you withheld the comma from your extreme punctuation; it became

"so you will benefit." We took a walk in the moonlight and were friends then
before our careers. Stop. The letter where we explain. Stop.

The lost body and tomb of Alexander the Great

Nabi Daniel — the Soma

Heuresis — finding of the lost body of Osiris

Césaire's *Corps perdu*:

"to the point of losing myself falling"

Electra: "not ever/to be there/with your lost body/
not ever/to wash you for the fire"

Mary Magdalene's "We do not know where they have laid him"

This process is used in the fabrication of rod, tubing, and wire

Soil which when unconfined has no significant cohesion when submerged

In an electric circuit, an on-off switch which can be actuated only
by the insertion of a key

Circular saw which is suspended from, and moves along, a cantilevered arm

Ornament consisting of a spirally wound band

Platform or small porch, usually up several steps

Dotted or a pebbly-textured finish on a surface coat of paint

Concrete in which the aggregate consists of exfoliated vermiculite

Any work, especially ornamental, characterized by perforations

DEAREST BODY:

I am not falling backwards

Some pre-solid self
rejecting this commerce
of the world —

Whether living alone
or living with another human —

Some primitive and infantile
force —

At least outwardly

Are you the instrumental one, the missing
twin, the one I lost and crave,
the beguiler — the fix?

Are you here simply —
for nothing other than to be
sunk into, discovered, lullabied, lamented —
united with, differentiated from?

Are you illusion, confusion, mis-
step, dream
mathematical equation
or poorly-worded conclusion?

X. writes me from her *pied-à-terre* on the outskirts of the city: *You see D. — the sun D. and the strategically drawn curtain reveals the absence of daylight.* It is purplish in the room blurring speech. I speak on the phone with X. who has not written me this morning. She breathes heavily between sentences, as if mourning the very continuity of thought. Evening is fully arrived. From inside, I can hear trucks accelerate and decelerate. The sound seems different. Indifferent.

I am currently researching an essay about bureaucracy and idealism. It will be published in the hotel dictionary. The rooms were so full there that we stayed instead at a friend's or slept in our car in the rear of the parking lot near the truckers. Rich experience, those years (as if our youth encased in clear plastic).

My body, my body, I do not seek to separate my head
from my heart, sweat from speech but to reprimand any who would
attempt such folly. Who could shun thee, when you allow your hand to
write out these
arguments to justify the existence of even
flawed things entering into the universe? Is it justifiable to negate you
because this same hand has been used to draft sinful denials?
So are these poems sinful in their own way. Is it
because they are born of some unhealthy alliance between
body and mind? Is it sufficient that the body at times
can be thought to overwrite the purity of consciousness?

The one thing I'll never forget about you

    is the one thing I most often forget about you

Head straining with
heartache now

Slicing through my meridian, the television in the night, and

everywhere else, like Broadway slightly sleazy —

    Secrets, blessed joy, grief

        falling through your dream
        into the present, then dialing

        up the manager as he flies off
        to some sacred place equidistant from all points

My brain, in this moment emotionless

    empty of theories, even
    that inference about owning a dog

A body, given free choice, would walk away
from everything he never knew,
unable to focus on this task

You beseech, and despite
your best efforts, continue to beseech.

And all doors close
when a star spins,
or so the story says.
I stay with you
because it took.
No word for this
in Latin or in song.
Eclipsed lips
darted outward.
You type out dreams
some say easily.
Others neglect
essential details
cut the deck
shuffle air.
What snow brought in.
Light for light's sake.

And it was never resolved, the hierarchy, the light, secret
data points, windows without curtains.

Codes that kiss your symmetry, a monotony of instinct.
Understanding how you came to this place

and how you'd leave it.
As a dream you took along whose words were playthings

swept the room in lovely waters.
A personal one whose hesitation was exhausted.

RE:

Around his thought, or a liquid
caress, something altogether contradictory.

Drunk and singing and laughing:
"I always drew the blinds

of my neighbors into late Modernist shadow."
Before she left, he would pretend she was not

his mistress — they are in a field
coloring in a fairy-tale house

and smoke opium like ephemeral buildings
necessitate their bed stays wide and low:

"It's over now" — with great feelings and violence of intention.
One felt deep down it made you cry

"how beautiful I am," as if caught between
a grotesque body and a deepening love.

I often swept into saying.
Wept over the unsaid sayings.
Slept in the loft of an
unknown artist.
I was hurt.
I was unhurt.
I sang into the wind.
There was no wind.
Whatever pain finally
became my anger.
Whatever anger
finally became my pain.
No longer material.
Metaphoric Rock.

If I sip tea and look for utopia in a lamp, it's not my existence that perplexes me it's your touch — graze of bone on skin — feel of space between the bone — nothingness you feel in vulnerable places — the thinness of every expression.

The idea of the two never existed because the idea of the one and the other paling in comparison to the one was omnipresent. The world was imbalanced and everything even the earth would fall to one side. However, in order to proceed you had to pretend that symmetry and therefore balance were indeed facts.

You type it out — to read it — now go home — the light
is on — this predicates an almost

documentary-like observation — the gray shifts — you are
looking at the sea again —

Suppose a text you wrote the very color of your skin became so laden
with the absolute it spun and wrapped you variably in its ethereal
nurturing

   Dear Body:

At the end of a string, how eyes discern
but never blend, making of an instinct. Ice
spread over snow.

     Man is a this if
     This if a is man
     A is if this man

I have forged ahead this nothing rhythm. Filmed your
talk of winter or sex.

Rocks picked out of sand examined.

       Water but none seemed as clear as

"I met my mind," you said
to which I replied "was that what you meant?"

ANTEBODIES

Writing a poem in six lines
is a miracle — come now!
Do you believe we can learn
truths about one another
through a series of mundane
exercises? I think not.

..

If I were to say to you
seven syllables — this is
my calling. A dance perhaps
or a liquid sentence — some
sentient being leave-behind
dark to the preparation.

...

Choir of three boys. Parts of
speech. Unordinary light.
Persian blinds preventing it.
The house running itself out
against the human race. Some
wish to transilluminate —

....

Transilluminate, or trans-
Atlantic. See through me to
a thin nausea of bone — less
inside than in the sacred
prose that allows ambition
(on this ocean of the lost).

·····

Will not candor feed unsaid,
the make believe winters blame,
an occurrence three times dead —
once in the avenue of
the bloody threads — once, under
fortune's ruinous heritage.

......

Hyper-real, the blue flower
inside this houseboat bent on
living. As if your open
suitcase spelled disappointment
with current conditions, or
suddenly the world's child

•••••••

Note: I never did these things:
a house on fire — running
out the door with a lost ring —
your door in splinters. Maybe
a twister caught your memory
in its pun — still, I wonder?

Without a champion, how
can we afford to die? It's
better to risk your passion
before impartial judges,
or at least anonymous
ones. What say you my lady?

....

These often lead to doubt. No
matter over mindfulness
can silence houses. Where I
stepped, I stepped. No silhouette
of fact can resuscitate
a dream gone rancid — partial.

··········

In the end, my deck of cards —
you see I didn't augment —
only a few islands drawn
in absurd detail — the rush
when something falls from your brain —
this is how it will occur

Ultimately just these. Not
a horticulture but an
I-can't-quake-in-its-mystique
sort of mystery. They say
he walks in the night after
a bar door creaks — no one's here.

An apartment (after all).
Never admitting she's down
here in a box, confused, torn,
motion of a motionless
particle, missing glass eye.
I heard all from my drawer.

．．．．．．．．．．．．．

Ok, another knot in
a disclosure empire
of thumbnail sketches. No, I
didn't — didn't know what seemed
to be my awarenesses
canceling out all belief.

I was not as concerned as
most. As if these questions pour
in and out of sense. It snowed
yesterday, plus or minus,
more or less. Several times
I meant to ask, but didn't.

Language on the wall, you say.
Porridge in this bowl to eat.
Vague markings on a column.
I want to go back to sleep.
You have no rights in this place.
Dare I mention my theory?

I would stare at the blank page,
drink a sip of coffee and
contemplate my ineptness.
Later, I got a call from
someone soliciting work
for an underground journal.

My lady does not live here.
She moved out to gain freedom.
Now she thinks the only way
to be a star is to be
thin. I hope she finds her dream
then. Meanwhile I'll be weeping.

Bless Juvenalius, the fool —
melancholic product of
his own forced seriousness.
Forgive his sophomoric truths
and wrap them in a blanket
for posterity's children.

Suddenly I was no one.
Not the loosely held ribbon;
or sand pouring through fingers;
or an uncle's beard I pulled.
Not my father's immense grip —
but the coolness of the sea.

As if forced into this form,
you cannot afford to fret.
Every modernism
falls perfectly into place.
I can't explain why structure
is good for man but it is.

Not here, not in a country
where sentimentality
has all but faded. This loss
must come from another place.
I cannot speak its name now —
but soon you will understand.

Afterwards, in his mature
voice, he spoke of natural
causes, qualities even
average people block out
from day-to-day existence
(strangely familiar theories).

Without being recognized —
slip away from daily life
into clouds of certain thoughts
you long ago banished. There —
someone will greet you with an
envelope containing truths.

Finally you were this thing
you couldn't make go away —
a thing with a certain weight
that hung over your thin frame.
It was a thinking being —
you stepped and it stepped also.

A few fragile things each day
for my motley collection
of sayings — some fall to the
bottom of my deepest drawer —
some remain perpetually
on my desk — ready for use.

No nuclear bomb went off
hidden in the fireworks.
No hand reached up and grabbed me
from deep beneath the lake moss.
I feel lucky I guess, lucky
for the insignificance.

Dark-green, late-blooming, subtle
trees, cars, wind, lake, apartments,
go, sit, bark, execute, sing,
congregate, trap, vaporize
hopes, intangibles, theories
unsubstantiated, vague.

ZERO: *Your eyes are green grass.*
EPITOME: *Not to mow?*
ZERO: *No. Wild grasses.*
EPITOME: *As if wheat?*
ZERO: *Then I would bake bread!*
EPITOME: *Sourdough?*

Before this I said nothing.
You can't escape from teachers,
and I've had mountains of them —
In the courtyard, the remnants
of the listeners stripped bare
of excuses — *my* move next?

EPITOME: *So he wept.*
ZERO: *And were there flowers?*
EPITOME: *No. Just rain.*
ZERO: *Then what can one say?*
EPITOME: *Nothing new.*
ZERO: *Except — of course — tears.*

I'm never alone with you.
Yesterday we even talked
half-believing of past lives —
I was a Jew in Poland
and my cat slipped into your
Swiss grandfather's herd of cows.

How you took a particle
and made it matter — always
innocently confessing
our lives were distinct in time —
your thinking to my thinking
— I have never forgotten.

I crave for poetic time —
that loss of silence in space —
what digital gurus scoff —
not clicks and permutations
but the between of daily
scenarios — equations.

Subitus, where did you go?
You were loved among poets.
You, who wrote the famous quip
about the professional
poet who loved the large dog
but let him die of neglect.

Artificialus, I
write this to your memory.
You of the plastic violence —
who looks pre-packaged in death.
Even you would admit that
uniqueness is a quaint myth.

When I am only waking,
I cannot dismiss my thoughts.
Your dreams become my genius
and I accept my morning,
a tiny emerging light
above a great tiredness.

Minus, you were so thin then —
under the tulip nothing
(where you recited visions).
I can't recall what I was
to you, stately underling
or boy who brought you water.

What you cannot ever say.
What you can't afford to say.
What happens before you sleep.
What you slip inside your mind.
What you dream never happened.
What you forget to write down.

I hope that you can see me,
you who look down at my face
from the government building.
Where you should go in the rain
is not because I told you
the impossible seconds.

ZERO: *You lost me before.*
EPITOME: *Over here.*
ZERO: *I meant your meaning.*
EPITOME: *So did I.*
ZERO: *Was it a left or . . .*
EPITOME: *You were right.*

What undid the house for us
above your porcelain chest?
What has the body left me?
Nothing, not even a song.
What's typically murmured
where I kiss your doll-like eyes.

It's not really important
whether poetry is red
or blue — I do it for fun.
Or because it doesn't hurt.
Or really because I'm scared
about nothing being done.

BEAUTIFUL LINEAR BODIES

This open destiny at love's expense —

I think blast through lake to wake a
brackish one —

The loggers destiny explains a transplant's aspiration

All I see is shrunken horizons

Going back to city's noise and air I might expire —

like all the memories I thought dead and (nevermind)

This tear of soup a glowing secret cork (and name paper burnt) — this tear
of blood the book names
writer's room a glistening wind glass mood or mudra

note the architecture black pus from a tree
idyllic photo of E. B. White's attic writing desk —
tear

of white flower (this grin to wake the past)
note to self:

Leonard Cohen — the writer's forgotten novel
(forgotten to me)

— year of the eye

two concentric points offering break note
out of simplistic vision was becoming a man killing things —

Leave New York and believe his name a mountain of fisheries

      holding a baby (the little man) or leaving a pasted hope or
    radio tower of babies — Jesus of Montreal (which I never saw
    but imagined)

      momentum of photo —
      wooden garner of poetry collection

Therapy the flowers

geese flouting beach wan up high tide

      half-burned grass full
      & summers together

            motorboat sunset *how to bear the sun*
            cold and wallow also writing here
            an expression (silence upon walking)

            fear palpable

      one bears

                the could would should

      putting out darkness — do not welcome thee *could I bury thee?*
      note the long-term hope this
      doting semblance

      little a. playing in the woods *loud this morning*
elsewhere the boards clamped in:

            meanwhile choreographing yellow notebook séances
              things dances some expression of mirth

. . . .

To *belong* become
Figurative dances
parking lots

A stop with love
or hate.
Or stone crabs —
Steve's seaweed briny smelling water.

Brakish lake or G.
don't break your foot in the woods with the cougars!

but animals will save you
(prints in the mud)

hysterical I even had my coffee and I'm weeping

(the blue distinct flowers)

George the George sailboat — *such a luxury*

for a G. — these are the prayers
no leaning robot sun

no diarist's yellow falling leaves in August

the linear as beautiful (which an east coast river escapes) — no song as sanded
pal — no hierarchy tree to tree —

as chain to chain
I unearthed what you could not say

the sea a
marketing plunger

take for profit what we wish
they won't catch us

fish a hardy lifestyle
that met shareholder approval

with our accounting
a semi-permanent thought

 — scrap of
wisdom traded down to

        & water-bullet sunlight

        rain, then radio —

        then a wind
        which is light like sex

        & treefrogs/toads
        So if the frogs are gone the environment's

        fucked —
        busy tabulating figures

        Hebrew or Sanskrit mouthing like English
        an abstract hope we think differently someday

the visible whitens in file box —
a period of half not open to food or categorized —

door closed due to AC and minor woes

I closet bake these sugar feelings and white you *au courant*

your break on life — the brazenness —
unspared look that B. would not have permitted

(or else laughed off)

there was a cult that rendered each religion infallible —

— so we took their note *blue-thick* and consequently a composing adventure —

if anyone exited out
a lining velvet I forgot

not that you would care you motherskates

our lease was up

off to see
Miami room

I drank it down

Go see Mulgrew Miller on a Tuesday —

    I was hoping they'd have some food there —

       the avoiding

                    gnawing at me — set

                   to rally and promise
                   rain down dog wind perish
          look I'm

    settling undisclosed his dinner frauds
    his pretty pen

    hero years reception lovingly going to

F train blessed in theory

             permission for your life

             reverify
             looking for a calendar

Y. at some literary bar we forgot —

                   what do I owe you?

       in faith like baptism (note the greenwood leaves) —

so few words

this is a love letter to _____ of 1979 (lost poet of history)

It was pitch black
and clap so loud the

sea unbuttoned
as those making wind

a frame coughed — also
blocked a man of breaks

 — tell me
is this, Primo, a man?

this hollow chest
a man whose almost is himself

a cabinet of curiosities
a man of bones, a lonely

cloister of Noh-masculinity
a living skeleton

an insignificant self —
I'm just lucky

I survived I think —
So all cells are superfluous

this bent up will
the will of flowers

Don't want to think of *it*
just give me money, paper, scissors

. . . .

Can't think the word evolves a flower by the shore — could not forget this a
blame or tide *red tide* the fad yesters or humpback islands point in distance —

His father abandoned him or living without one physically (or the green gray
ocean) — her father: *a legendary trapper*

see form & not withstanding this and that being without me
thistle blatantly or borne in time a blaze looked

                              and shone
                              on upper-forehead
                              turned left at bush
                              and blackberry storms

                              homes — made ice — its

                              unprecedented slight wind fishy
                              smell

What's back in the window with exclamation point wavering — forget the
example (pie in the face) a tree windows open upon landing

what is your Icelandic book Felix?

point of obnoxiousness the discipline of radical monkhood
ok this day a kept man or woman
my 3 pages

a disciple like me virtually
a bikeride
this open sesame for purple Venuses

dear gray phenomenal island:

alone again
mystery and saying periods
of love and song
blue and holiday

alone
in the wheel

little a.'s voice like a tiny
merboy by the water —

an old propane tank
(who knows how safe?)

I rack my mind
is sandalwood

— the blaze
is where I read

a red zero to her
up a bed of flowers

don't step on the bed
your sleep unhappy

enough to wake sunlight
reactionary still

a data point

already fall resolves —
I wet my mind

in distance

or else strikes a clock bell —

what sparkles courage into the riffraff of density
courage — being literal in timeframe — no insignificant mood

depth of *I am* over the top wrong and also right — sour flavor

it's still Guinness though there is no Guinness
best in doing what instinct does best — this understanding

who to publish? For example —
his greatest evening skating by an interest in sense

grace and figuration
mixes it (and the three-

legged dog hobbles over
his hit-by-a-car look
of sadness but he deals) —

to be alive and dream the
unforgettable houseboats of terrible movies?

I consider myself very likeable — Tzara

    At Kasbah Willy's
    glance your leave

    punching dump trucks not just killing time
    time is wet work

is fun — a radium dial or a wet and sinewy ok

ACKNOWLEDGMENTS

Many thanks to Matvei, Anna, Genya, Greg, Ryan, Phil, Garth, Nalini and all the other members of the UDP collective for their care in publishing this book and a previous limited edition chapbook, *6x7*.

Many thanks to the following magazines who published earlier versions of some of these poems: *Fence* — "Letter 1," "Letter 2," "Thursday Letter," "Letter to D."; *Tarpaulin Sky* — "Fifth Letter," "Letter in Which We Type These Letters," "Letter of Intent"; Soft Targets — "Letter of Critique," "Dear Body," "29th Letter," "Letter in Which It Is Explained"; *ArtVoice* (Buffalo) — "Letter from Quebec"; *Antennae* — "Writing a book," "Choir of three boys," "Note I never," "Finally you were," "Without a champion"; *Boog Lit* — "Language on the wall"; *Café Review* — selections from "Beautiful Linear Bodies."

Much appreciation for the wisdom and encouragement of the many readers of this manuscript and work in earlier forms, most notably Jen Hofer, Laird Hunt, Rachel Levitsky, and especially Garrett Kalleberg. Finally, thanks to the Machlin and Jost families, and to all my friends and many wonderful teachers without whom this work would not have been possible.

ABOUT THE AUTHOR

Dan Machlin was born and raised in New York City. Previous works include several chapbooks: *6x7* (Ugly Duckling Presse), *This Side Facing You* (Heart Hammer Press), and *In Rem* (@ Press), as well as *Above Islands* (Immanent Audio), an audio CD collaboration with singer/cellist Serena Jost. His poems and reviews have appeared in *Fence, The Poetry Project Newsletter, Talisman, Antennae, Crayon, Soft Targets, Cy Press, Boog Literature* and *The Brooklyn Rail*. Dan is the founding editor and publisher of Futurepoem books, a former contributing editor of *The Transcendental Friend* and a former co-curator of The Segue Series at Bowery Poetry Club in NYC. *Dear Body:* is his first book-length collection of poems.

COLOPHON

This is the first edition of *Dear Body:* by Dan Machlin.

Design by Don't Look Now.

Text set in Caslon. Titles set in Helvetica Neue.

Covers printed offset by Polyprint Design (www.polyprintdesign.com)
on Fabriano Murillo paper.

Books printed on acid-free Finch opaque vellum and bound by Bookmobile
(www.bookmobile.com).